What if......there had been World W...

#Berlin45

The Final Days of the Third Reich told in the form of Twitter feeds

The compelling story of the final 20 days of Hitler's Third Reich told in the form of Twitter feeds with daily tweets and actual statements by Hitler, Churchill, Truman, Zhukov, Eisenhower, Goebbels, Bormann, Weidling, Krebs, Keitel, Jodl, Patton, Bradley, Heinrici, Konev, Chuikov, Eva Braun and many others.

The story begins with the announcement of, and reactions to, the death of President Franklin D. Roosevelt and follows the thoughts and actions of the main participants through the capture of Vienna, the Battle of Seelow Heights, the liberation of the concentration camps, the Battle of Berlin, the death of Hitler and the eventual surrender of Reich forces.

by Philip Gibson

Thursday
12 April, 1945

WHITE HOUSE @Whitehouse
President died of cerebral hemorrhage this afternoon at Warm Springs, Ga. VP notified. State has been advised. Cabinet meeting called.

Harry S. Truman @Truman
Going to meet Sam Rayburn, but told to go to the White House where I was informed of the President's death. Sworn in as President at about 7 p.m.

Winston Churchill @Churchill
Tragic news! I feel I have been struck a physical blow!

Joseph Goebbels @JGoebbels
Heard this news and saw the Angel of History - felt its wings flutter through the room. Is this not the future we have awaited so anxiously?

George Patton @Patton
Visited Ohrdruf work camp with Brad and Ike. Sickening what these Nazi bastards did there. It was all I could manage not to throw up.

George Patton @Patton
Just heard the news of FDR's death on the BBC radio. Unpleasant day all round!

Joseph Goebbels @Goebbels
Have informed the Führer of the good news. He is beside himself with joy! What glorious intervention! What future for National Socialism!

Joseph Stalin @JStalin
Received news of the President's death. I have ordered his picture be printed on the front page of every Russian newspaper tomorrow.

Adolf Hitler @AHitler
Goebbels has informed me of the death of Roosevelt - portent of the ultimate victory of National Socialism and the defeat of the Bolsheviks.

Winston Churchill @Churchill
Grieving the loss of a warm-hearted friend! The world has lost a very great man - the foremost champion of the high causes we both served.

Adolf Hitler @AHitler
Such events do not occur by happenstance, but are mandated by the gods of destiny!

Joseph Stalin @JStalin
Marshal Zhukov sends me more good news this day. Our Great Patriotic War nears its final glorious moments!

Winston Churchill @Churchill
Stalin has informed me that he expects Vienna to fall by the weekend. Would that FDR had lived to hear of this.

New York Times @DCNYT
Last words of the late President: "I have a terrific pain in the back of my head!"

Eleanor Roosevelt @EleanorR
Harry asked if there was anything he could do for me. I replied, "Is there anything we can do for you? You are the one in trouble now."

Friday
13 April, 1945

Winston Churchill (1874-1965)

Winston Churchill was Prime Minister of Great Britain during most of World War II. His steadfast refusal to consider defeat, surrender, or a compromise peace helped inspire British resistance, especially during the difficult early days of the War when Britain stood alone among European countries in its active opposition to Adolf Hitler.

Winston Churchill @Churchill
I have sent a telegram of condolences to Franklin's widow. Expect to talk to President Truman later today.

Pravda @YuriPravda
Just interviewed Marshal Tolbukhin who told me plans for the final assault on Vienna are now complete.

Adolf Hitler @AHitler
I have ordered General Bittrich to hold Vienna to the last breath.

Harry S. Truman @Truman
I have just met with a bunch of reporters and told them frankly that I feel like the moon, the stars and all the planets have fallen on me!

Fyodor Tolbukhin @Fyodor
Following my detailed plans forwarded to Col. General Stoychev earlier today, I expect the Bulgarian army to have taken Vienna by day's end.

Vladimir Stoychev @Stoychev
The Germans have destroyed several Danube bridges as they retreat. Reichbrucke Bridge is still intact.

Harry Truman @Truman
About to be briefed by Secretary of War Stimson on progress on Western/Eastern fronts and other war matters.

Wilhelm Bittrich @WBittrich
I have told Von Bunau to hold Reichbrucke Bridge as long as possible but to withdraw and demolish bridge at his discretion.

Vladimir Stoychev @Stoychev
Troops landed on both sides of Reichbrucke Bridge and are cutting demolition cables

Heinrich Himmler @HH
Loyalty of Bittrich to the Führer has long been questionable. No reason to expect he will obey the Führer's commands re. defense of Vienna.

Rudolf von Bunau @ RDB
Enemy now over the Danube in numbers. Reichbrucke Bridge taken. Sector cannot hold. Requesting permission to withdraw from sector.

Fyodor Tolbukhin @Fyodor
Danube canals successfully stormed. Reichbrucke Bridge captured. Armor advancing. Expect complete occupation of Vienna by Sunday latest.

Wilhelm Bittrich @WBittrich
I will pull out II SS Panzer Corps to the west this evening to avoid encirclement.

Vladimir Stoychev @Stoychev
Reports from troops entering city centre: no water, electricity or gas anywhere in Vienna now.

Wilhelm Bittrich @WBittrich
No chance now to hold Vienna. Have informed Berlin of withdrawal details. Awaiting reply/further orders.

Vladimir Stoychev @Stoychev
No police in evidence in Vienna now. Bands of people (Both foreigners and Austrians) are plundering and raping residents.

Heinrich Himmler @HH
I'm hearing that General Bittrich and General von Bunau have both left Vienna to avoid capture by the Soviets.

Helmuth Weidling @HWeidling
I have been appointed commander of the LVI Panzer Corps in Army Group Vistula. The sombre task is to deliver the capital from the Soviets.

Heinrich Himmler @HH
The Führer should have replaced Bittrich a year ago as I advised.

Pravda @YuriPravda
BREAKING NEWS: Vienna has fallen to the Red Army!

Saturday 14 April, 1945

Heinrich Himmler (1900-1945)

Himmler was Head of the SS, a military commander and leading member of the Nazi Party. One of the most powerful men in Germany during World War II, and one of the persons most directly responsible for the Holocaust.

Heinrich Himmler @HH
I have ordered Col. Bercher to negotiate the surrender of Dachau and other camps.

Reuters @Reuters
In Italy, General Truscott's Fifth Army continues to press forward in the direction of Bologna.

Lucian K. Truscott @Truscott
We have captured Massa and crossed the Frigido River after considerable German resistance in the mountains.

Reuters @Reuters
US Ninth Army discovered corpses of over 1,000 prisoners shot and burned to death in a barn outside the town of Gardelegen in eastern Germany.

Lucian K. Truscott @Truscott
Moving on to Bologna.

Reuters @Reuters
The American advance has split the Ruhr pocket in two as troops of the 1st and 9th Armies meet at the town of Hagen in the heart of the Ruhr.

Heinrich Himmler @HH
Cancelled order to Bercher. Dachau camp must be evacuated immediately. No prisoner must be allowed to fall into the hands of the enemy alive.

New York Times @DCNYT
In Italy, the US Fifth Army has the Germans up against the Po river where they continue to fight despite having few heavy weapons.

Lucian K. Truscott @Truscott
II Corps are through Milan and nearing the French border. IV Corps have linked up with the Seventh Army at the Brenner Pass.

Adolf Hitler @AHitler
The Southern Front was never a viable option for the Anglo-Americans, and sending our forces to defend it was a bad idea that I resisted.

Sunday
15 April, 1945

Richard Dimbleby (1913-1965)

Richard Dimbleby was a BBC journalist. He accompanied the British Expeditionary Force to France, made broadcasts from the Battle of El Alamein and the Normandy beaches during the D-Day landings. In 1945, he broadcast the first reports from Belsen Concentration Camp.

Richard Dimbleby @BBCDimbleby
We are approaching a German concentration camp near the town of Bergen. I have been told to prepare to be appalled.

New York Times @DCNYT
The completely exhausted remnants of what had been the 6th SS Panzer Army have been forced to flee to the area between Vienna and Linz.

Joseph Kramer @JKramer
Bergen-Belsen Camp now holds upwards of 60,000 inmates, with an additional 28,000 transferred here just this week. Situation is intolerable!

New York Times @DCNYT
None of these German armies is in any shape to do more than temporarily stall the rapidly advancing Soviet forces.

Pravda @YuriPravda
Do not count the days! Do not count the miles! Count only the Germans you have killed. Kill the German! This is your old mother's prayer.

Reuters @PGReuters
Reports of heavy fighting near Winsen and Walle, Northwestern Germany.

Eva Braun @EBraun
I have no greater wish than to be at the side of the Führer in this difficult time. I have accordingly taken a residence in the Führerbunker.

Joseph Stalin @Stalin
Zhukov reports further gains. German resistance is crumbing before the heroic Red Army advance.

Reuters @PGReuters

The British 11th. Armoured Division have entered a concentration camp southwest of the town of Bergen in northwestern Germany.

Joseph Kramer @JKramer
The British have arrived at our camp. I have therefore surrendered authority and taken their senior officers on a tour of our facilities.

Trudl Junge @TJunge
Fraulein Braun has today joined us in the Führerbunker. I do so hope that this will lighten the Führer's mood which has become so dark of late.

Richard Dimbleby @BBCDimbleby
Here in Belsen Concentration Camp, over an acre of ground lay dead and dying people. You can not see which is which!

Joseph Kramer @JKramer
The British had agreed to let me stay on as Camp Commandant to uphold order inside the camp. Now they say I am to be arrested and tried.

Richard Dimbleby @BBCDimbleby
The living here in Belsen camp lay, emaciated, aimless, with their heads against the corpses. The scenes here are the stuff of nightmares!

Richard Dimbleby @BBCDimbleby
This day at the Belsen concentration camp has been the most horrible day of my life!

Monday
16 April, 1945

Georgi Zhukov (1896-1974)

Deputy Supreme Commander of all Soviet Forces. Marshal Zhukov was a Soviet career officer in the Red Army who played a pivotal role in the defense of the Soviet Union and leading the Red Army drive through much of Eastern Europe to capture the German capital and ensure the demise of Nazi Germany. He is the most decorated officer in the history of the Soviet Union and Russia.

Georgi Zhukov @Zhukov
While confident of victory in our march towards Berlin, we have to ensure this offensive is not only 100% successful, but 200% successful!

Adolf Hitler @AHitler
The Jewish Bolshevik enemy is attacking for the last time. The Bolshevik will experience Asia's old fate - he must, and will, bleed to death.

Pravda @YuriPravda
I am with the 1st Belorussian Front from where Marshal Zhukov is expected to launch the assault on 'the Gates of Berlin' imminently.

Gotthard Heinrici @GHeinrici
I am convinced the Soviets will attempt a mass crossing of the Oder within this day.

Theodor Busse @TBusse
I am awaiting final orders from General Heinrici.

Gotthard Heinrici @Heinrici
General Busse has completed fortification of Seelow Heights overlooking both the river and the autobahn.

Georgi Zhukov @Zhukov
With nearly 80,000 troops of the Polish 1st Army, we are now close to 1 million strong heading to the 'Gates of Berlin'.

Theodor Busse @TBusse
We have completed three lines of defenses behind the Heights, spreading back toward Berlin.

Gotthard Heinrici @Heinrici
We are facing a million-man Soviet force with only 110,000 soldiers of the German 9th Army. May God help us and protect the Fatherland!

Theodor Busse @TBusse
Our defensive lines now consist of anti-tank ditches, anti-tank gun emplacements, and an extensive network of trenches and bunkers.

Gotthard Heinrici @Heinrici
I have ordered Busse to withdraw defenders from the first line of trenches – too vulnerable to Soviet artillery.

Theodor Busse @TBusse
Our lines are now under a massive bombardment by thousands of Soviet artillery pieces and Katyushas.

Georgi Zhukov @Zhukov
Progress is too slow. I am sending in reserves.

Joseph Stalin @JStalin
I have told Zhukov that I will let Konev direct his tank armies north, toward the great prize of Berlin.

Gotthard Heinrici @Heinrici
With no reinforcements, we can only hold the Heights for 3 or 4 days at most. And OKH inform me that no reinforcements are available.

New York Times @NYT
While the Red Army is making serious inroads in the east, the German forces in the Ruhr eastern pocket are surrendering in their thousands.

Walter Model @WModel
I have discharged the oldest and youngest soldiers in Army Group B. The remainder may surrender or attempt to break out on their own.

Joseph Goebbels @JGoebbels
Field Marshal Model has dissolved his army in the Ruhr rather than surrendering. Is such an action any less treacherous?

Walter Model @WModel
What can there be left for a commander in defeat? In antiquity, they took poison. For myself, I choose the pistol.

Tuesday
17 April, 1945

Gotthard Heinrici (1886-1971)

Senior general in the German army during World War II. Considered one of the best defensive tacticians in the German Army, leading to his final assignment as Commander in Chief of the last remaining forces of Army Group Vistula (final remnants of Army Group Center) in front of Berlin in April 1945.

Gotthard Heinrici @GHeinrici
Schörner informs me Army Group Centre has been further weakened and no longer able to mount a viable defense.

Wilhelm Keitel @WKeitel
What remain of our forces in the western pocket of the Ruhr have also surrendered to the Americans.

Pravda @YuriPravda
On this second day of the Battle for Seelow Heights, the 1st Belorussian Front continues to advance in accordance with Marshal Zhukov's plan.

Martin Bormann @MBormann
The Führer flew into a rage on hearing the disgraceful news of Model's army in the Ruhr. He is now calm once again.

Adolf Hitler @AHitler
I expected more of Model. However, it is towards the east that we must concentrate all effort. I no longer worry about the Anglo-Americans.

Georgi Zhukov @Zhukov
Battle plan back on schedule. We are attacking the second German defensive line with massive force and expect to have broken it by evening.

Joseph Stalin @Stalin
Marshal Chuikov continues to argue that Zhukov is too cautious. He believes we could have entered Berlin weeks ago.

Martin Bormann @MBormann
What remain of Army Group Vistula are mounting a heroic defense of the Heights, but I fear it is futile.

Joseph Goebbels @JGoebbels
I have full faith that Schoerner will lead Army Group Center to a successful defense, gaining the Führer the time needed to re-organize.

Wilhelm Keitel @WKeitel
A total of more than 300,000 German soldiers in the Ruhr have surrendered. How can I tell this to the Führer?

Georgi Zhukov @Zhukov
German 2nd defensive line broken and 11th Tank Corp advancing.

Gotthard Heinrici @GHeinrici
More Soviet troops have crossed the river. Our defensive lines are exposed and being strafed by Soviet aircraft.

Georgi Zhukov @Zhukov
The second German defensive line has been thoroughly smashed. The 47th. and 3rd. Shock Armies have progressed a further 4-8 kilometers.

Gotthard Heinrici
Third defensive line is holding out for now – inflicting heavy losses on the approaching Soviets.

Alfred Jodl @AJodl
If Heinrici and Schoeder are unable to hold back the Soviets now, what hope can there be for any viable defense of Berlin?

Wednesday 18 April, 1945

Alfred Jodl (1890-1946)

Jodl was Chief of the Operations Staff of the Armed Forces High Command (OKW) during World War II acting as deputy to Wilhelm Keitel. He signed the official unconditional surrender of Germany as a representative for German president Karl Doenitz.

Alfred Jodl @AJodl
I had to inform General Heinrici that there is no possibility of sending significant reinforcements. Such a contingency was not planned for.

Pravda @YuriPravda
I witness this day possibly the heaviest artillery onslaught in history – directed against the last line of defense at the 'Gates of Berlin'.

Alfred Jodl @AJodl
Our defensive lines at the Seelow Heights are paying the price for the Führer's refusal to transfer units from the western front.

Joseph Stalin @Stalin
Marshals Zhukov and Konev have made similar progress. Soon we will see which commander deserves the right to take the prize of Berlin.

Gotthard Heinrici @GHeinrici
The Soviets began this offensive with an advantage of 11, 7 and 20 to 1 in men, tanks and guns respectively. This was an impossible defense!

Alfred Jodl @AJodl
There has long been no constructive communication between the generals and the Führer. And what little there is goes through Bormann.

Winston Churchill @Churchill
Recent advances on all fronts leave me in no doubt whatsoever that victory in Europe is assured - the task now is to prepare for peace.

Pravda @YuriPravda
Despite very heavy losses, the 1st Belorussian Front has reached the third and final German line of defense below the Seelow Heights.

Martin Bormann @MBormann
General Heinrici reports that the third line at Seelow Heights is about to collapse. He requests permission to withdraw.

Theodor Busse @TBusse
The Soviet tanks which have broken through our third defensive line are unable to mount the steep slopes of the Heights. We hold on...for now.

Alfred Jodl @AJodl
During this past year, the Führer has replaced the entire leadership on the eastern front for one reason or another. Heinrici may be next.

George S. Patton @Patton
If I were Ike, I'd have insisted we take Berlin ourselves. And having taken it, we should continue to fight eastwards...all the way to Moscow!

Joseph Stalin @Stalin
I have informed Konev that he need not wait for Zhukov, but is to turn his two tank armies north towards Berlin.

Alfred Jodl @AJodl
If Soviet tanks are to roll into Berlin, are we to rely on the infirm, young boys, and old men of the Volkssturm to save the capital?

Heinrich Himmler @HH
The Volkssturm may lack military experience, but that is made up for in ideological purity and Party loyalty. Unlike many of our generals!

Gotthard Heinrici @GHeinrici
Schörner's defenses to the south of the Heights were inadequate. Our positions become more untenable every hour.

Pravda @YuriPravda
The 1st. Ukranian Front of Marshal Konev continues to push forward, causing the left flank of Army Group Center to crumble.

Gotthard Heinrici @GHeinrici
If Army Group Vistula and Army Group Center do not pull back immediately, we will face envelopment. We must pull back!

Thursday
19 April, 1945

Joseph Stalin (1878-1953)

Often referred to as Marshal Stalin, he was the leader of the Soviet Union before, during and after World War II. After entering into a non-aggression pact with Nazi Germany, from 1941 to 1945 he oversaw the defense of the Soviet Union and eventual victory of the Red Army over Nazi Germany.

Joseph Stalin @Stalin
Just days from now, before Labor Day, our forces will be in the lair of the fascist beast and hoisting the Soviet flag above his Reichstag.

Joseph Goebbels @JGoebbels
I have instructed my Ministry to announce tomorrow that Model and his entire Army Group B are officially designated as traitors to the Reich.

Ivan Konev @Konev
Armies under my command were the first to advance onto German soil, and I am now the first to turn my armies to enter the German capital.

Alfred Jodl @AJodl
Schörner's Army Group Center is collapsing and the position of Army Group Vistula has become untenable.

Pravda @YuriPravda
The Armies of the 1st Ukrainian Front are racing west toward the Americans. The German eastern front line no longer exists.

Hans Krebs @HKrebs
Huge sections of the 9th. Army and 4th. Panzer have been enveloped by the two Red Army fronts in a large pocket 37 km. east of Frankfurt.

Pravda @YuriPravda
Marshall Zhukov has broken through the final line of the German defenses. Only broken Reich formations now lay between his armies and Berlin.

Alfred Jodl @AJodl
What little remain of the 9th Army and the 4th Panzer Army are now enveloped by the Soviets who have broken through and turned toward Berlin.

Pravda @YuriPravda
General Weidling's LVI Panzer Corps are now retreating back towards Berlin.

Alfred Jodl @AJodl
Our front line in the east has ceased to exist. All that remain are disorganized pockets of resistance.

Georgi Zhukov @Zhukov
Heinrici makes no further attempt at defense. I am able to advance while ignoring what remains of Army Group Vistula.

Hans Krebs @HKrebs
I have informed Bormann that units of Marshal Konev's Ukranian Front have broken through and turned north towards Berlin.

Pravda @YuriPravda
The German defensive line on the Seelow Heights was the last major defensive line outside Berlin. The road to Berlin now lays open!

Alfred Jodl @AJodl
General Heinrici pulled back what he could of his forces, including Weidling's LVI Panzer Corps.

Heinrich Himmler @HH
Is General Heinrici no longer cognizant of the fact that no retreat can be authorized without the personal approval of the Führer?

Georgi Zhukov @Zhukov
The road to Berlin (90 km to the west) now lays open before me. However, Konev's armies will have a similar opportunity.

Heinrich Himmler @HH
The Führer has issued no approval for withdrawal. Heinrici is acting in brazen defiance of standing orders and his oath to the Führer!

Joseph Stalin @JStalin
German defenses have now been utterly smashed. Both Zhukov and Konev are advancing to take Berlin. But only one of them shall have the prize.

Friday
20 April, 1945

Hans Krebs (1898-1945)

German Army Infantry General who was Chief of the Army General Staff (OKH) in the latter stages of World War II.

Hans Krebs @HKrebs
The Belorussian and Ukranian Fronts are approaching from the east/northeast and south respectively – largely unopposed.

Reuters @DCReuters
Today is Adolf Hitler's 56th birthday.

Alfred Jodl @HJodl
The government district is now under Soviet artillery fire for the first time. The Reichstag has been hit.

Martin Bormann @MBormann
General Krebs informs me that the US 7th. Army has captured Nuremberg.

Joseph Goebbels @JGoebbels
Today is the birthday of our Führer: a man of unparalleled courage, of a steadfastness that uplifts hearts and spirits!

Wilhelm Keitel @WKeitel
This morning, together with my wife and Dönitz, I watched over 1,000 American bombers pound our capital – with no response from our side.

Reuters @DCReuters
Soldiers of the 3rd, 42nd and 45th Infantry Divisions of the US Seventh Army celebrate taking of Nuremberg - capital of German nationalism.

Joseph Stalin @Stalin
Marshals Zhukov and Konev and our glorious Red Army will ensure this is the last birthday Hitler spends on his own terms.

Hans Krebs @HJodl
Himmler, Keitel and Bormann are trying to persuade the Führer to leave for the Obersalzberg to lead the Great German Resistance.

Eva Braun @EBraun
The Führer asked that no special celebrations be held during this austere time, but the secretaries and I are preparing a surprise for him.

Dwight D. Eisenhower @Eisenhower
This morning's bombing raid on Berlin will be the last now that the Red Army are about to enter the city.

Alfred Jodl @AJodl
With much of the Wehrmacht incapacitated, we now depend on the very young and the very old of the Volkssturm to defend the capital.

Adolf Hitler @AHitler
I went outside the Führerbunker to meet boys of the Hitler Youth defending our capital. Brave, brave boys! Pride of our Fatherland!

Richard Dimbleby @BBCDimbleby
Reports say Marshal Konev's forces to the south of Berlin have taken more than 10,000 German prisoners in the past four days.

Adolf Hitler @AHitler
I awarded several iron crosses to those young boys of the Volkssturm. They are far more deserving of such honor than my cowardly generals!

Joseph Goebbels @JGoebbels
On a day when many would be enjoying the good wishes of their friends and family, the Führer continues to work diligently for the Fatherland.

Hans Krebs @HKrebs
The Führer has informed us that he will remain in the Führerbunker until the end.

Joseph Goebbels @JGoebbels
Our Führer was born from the womb of the German people who raised him onto their shield in a free election: a man of truly secular greatness!

Gotthard Heinrici @GHeinrici
Unless the 9th. Army moves further west immediately, it will be completely enveloped by the Soviets.

Richard Dimbleby @BBCDimbleby
Marshal Zhukov's troops, heading to Berlin from the north and east, claim to have taken more than 13,000 prisoners and captured 60 aircraft.

Wilhelm Keitel @WKeital
If Germany is cut in two by the drive of the armies from the east and the west, then Dönitz should take charge of the defenses in the north.

Gotthard Heinrici @GHeinrici
I will tell Bormann that if the Führer does not allow the 9th. Army to move further west, I will ask to be relieved of my command.

Trudle Junge @TJunge
Many staff have left. Today, for the first time, we have started to think we may be defeated and trapped in Berlin.

Saturday 21 April, 1945

Martin Bormann (1900-1945)

Bormann was Head of the Party Chancellery and Private Secretary to Hitler. He had immense power due to his position conveying Hitler's orders and controlling the flow of information to and from Hitler.

Martin Bormann @MBormann
This morning, the sounds of incessant Soviet artillery shelling are clearly heard even down here in the Führerbunker.

Pravda @YuriPravda
Today we see the opening stages of what history will record as the final days of 'the Battle of Berlin'.

Joseph Stalin @Stalin
Both Zhukov and Konev are launching multiple assaults on German positions both in and around the Reich capital.

Hans Krebs @HKrebs
Artillery shells are now falling in the city center and close to the Reich Chancellery. The Führer continues to forbid discussion of evacuation.

Martin Borman @MBorman
In addition to this morning's Soviet shelling, the capital has now suffered 36 nights in succession of bombing raids by the British.

Alfred Jodl @AJodl
General Heinrici has informed Bormann that unless the Führer allows the 9th. Army to retreat west, he will ask to be relieved of his command.

Joseph Goebbels @JGoebbels
Heinrici continues his cowardly retreat and now requests that his new headquarters be established WEST of the capital!

Martin Bormann @MBormann
A third Soviet front has just overrun more of our defenses positioned north of Berlin.

Wilhelm Keitel @WKeitel

I have implored the Führer to allow the 9th. Army to retreat in order to avoid its total destruction.

Adolf Hitler @AHitler
The 9th. Army will not withdraw further! Heinrici has his orders. It is clear! I have told him and Busse to fight where they stand!

Hans Krebs @HKrebs
The IV Panzer Army are reporting some success attacking north to counter advances by the 1st. Ukrainian Front.

Adolf Hitler @AHitler
Steiner's unit must attack from the north, meet up with the 9th. Army and crush the Soviets with a relentless and mighty assault!

Alfred Jodl @AJodl
Army Detachment Steiner is worn out, exhausted and outnumbered ten to one.

Adolf Hitler @AHitler
Wenck's 12th. Army will provide General Steiner all necessary support.

Alfred Jodl @AJodl
The 12th. Army is defending the western front. However, the Führer has insisted that it be turned around immediately.

Adolf Hitler @AHitler
The orders to Steiner are clear. He must attack, without delay, the 1st Belorussian Front and destroy it without regard to mercy.

Alfred Jodl @AJodl

There is no possibility of the 9th. Army being in a position to support the attack by Steiner that the Führer has ordered.

Adolf Hitler @Ahitler
General Jodl continues to question my decisions and orders. Does he not realize that I have conquered all of Europe – on my own!

Alfred Jodl @AJodl
SS-General Steiner has only a few operational tanks and roughly a division's worth of infantry. What does the Führer expect of him?

Hans Krebs @HKrebs
Mohnke requested the evacuation of women, children and the elderly. The Führer refused, saying they had chosen this outcome themselves.

Adolf Hitler @AHitler
We cannot worry ourselves concerning the fate of these so-called citizens. In a war such as this - a total war - there are no civilians!

Hans Krebs @HKrebs
The Führer does not appreciate that what remain of the units available to Steiner are themselves facing encirclement and annihilation.

Alfred Jodl @AJodl
The orders given by the Führer today reflect the fact that he has totally lost any understanding of the real situation!

Adolf Hitler @AHitler
It is neither possible, nor will it be permitted, for those cultureless Bolshevik barbarians to conquer Europe!

Adolf Hitler @AHitler
I am the last bastion against the Bolshevik threat! The only hope for Europe!

Joseph Goebbels @JGoebbels
The Führer is correct! Only here in Berlin, from this bunker, can moral victory be achieved!

Alfred Jodl @AJodl
These orders are irrational. However, we have no choice but to remain loyal and forward the commands of the Führer.

Hans Krebs @HKrebs
Steiner reports he does not have the divisions to carry out the orders to attack the 1st. Belorussian Front and asks permission to retreat.

Martin Bormann @MBormann
Who will inform the Führer of SS-General Steiner's reply? At any rate, it can wait until tomorrow. Enough of this day!

Sunday
22 April, 1945

Wilhelm Keitel (1882-1946)

Keitel was German Field Marshall and Head of the Supreme Command of the Armed Forces. Effectively Minister of War under Hitler.

Wilhelm Keitel @WKeitel
After this meeting I will drive to General Wenck's HQ to relay the Führer's exact orders for the 12th. Army to move to the defense of Berlin.

Adolf Hitler @AHitler
I have ordered that General Weidling be executed by firing squad for retreating from battle in defiance of my orders to stand and fight.

Hans Krebs @HKrebs
Today, I had to inform the Führer that the enemy has broken through on a wide front and many of the suburbs are under attack.

Adolf Hitler @AHitler
Krebs exaggerates the difficulties. When SS-General Steiner attacks, that will bring the situation under control.

Alfred Jodl @AJodl
It fell to me to inform the Führer that General Steiner cannot raise the forces to mount an attack.

Adolf Hitler @AHitler
Steiner's assault was an order! Who are these generals that they dare disobey an order that I give?

Alfred Jodl @AJodl
I felt it wise not to inform the Führer that Steiner has also requested permission to withdraw. Such news would only enrage him further.

Adolf Hitler @AHitler
For years, the military have hindered my plans! The generals and senior officers are traitors and failures!

Adolf Hitler @AHitler
The military, everybody, has been lying to me. Even the SS! Under these circumstances, I am no longer able to lead. It's over!

Wilhelm Keitel @WKeitel
The Führer was beside himself at the withdrawal of Heinrici and Steiner! This is the first time he has voiced a view that the war is lost.

Adolf Hitler @AHitler
What I should have done is liquidate all the high-ranking military officers, as Stalin did!

Alfred Jodl @AJodl
The Führer's tirade and abuse of the German army and its generals during today's meeting was outrageous!

Hans Krebs @HKrebs
The Führer has become totally despondent. He has given all of us permission to leave Berlin should we wish.

Martin Bormann @MBormann
This afternoon comes news that Soviet troops have penetrated the inner line around Berlin and are now less than 8 miles from the Chancellery.

Adolf Hitler @AHitler
If the German people are to lose the war, it is because they are the weaker ones. I will not shed a tear for them!

Wilhelm Keitel @WKeitel

During today's situation conference, the Führer launched into a dreadful rage the like of which I have never seen before.

Trudle Junge @TJunge
Hans told me that the Führer actually wept tears of rage during the conference in the Führerbunker today.

Martin Bormann @MBormann
Against our advice, the Führer continues to be adamant that he will remain in Berlin to head up the defense of the capital.

Eva Braun @EBraun
The Führer told us that there would be a plane to transport us safely out of Berlin within the hour. I refused to leave his side.

Adolf Hitler @AHitler
Eva and my secretaries have refused to leave Berlin despite the immense danger bearing down on us. If only my generals were as brave!

Trudl Junge @FJunge
The Führer announced that all is now lost. When Eva refused to leave him, he kissed her on the lips. The only time we have seen such a thing.

Joseph Goebbels @JGoebbels
The people chose, in a free vote, to reject a policy of subordination and in favor of a bold gamble. They deserve the fate that awaits them.

Martin Bormann @MBormann
Keitel is on his way to instruct Wenck to disengage with the Americans and attack to the east to link up with Busse's Army.

Hans Krebs @HKrebs
Wenck and Busse are to attack the Soviets from the west and south. General Holste will attack from the north.

Alfred Jodl @AJodl
The forces of General Holste amount to little. They largely consist of transfers from General Steiner's depleted units.

Martin Bormann @MBormann
Following the noon meeting, the Führer ordered relocation of most of the military staff to Goering at the Obersalzberg.

Hans Krebs @HKrebs
This evening, the Führer appointed me representative of the supreme commander of the Wehrmacht in the Führerbunker.

Hans Krebs @HKrebs
SS-General Mohnke is to be commander of the defense of the government sector.

Joseph Goebbels @JGoebbels
My faithful Magda and our six children have joined their beloved 'Uncle Adolf' and myself in the Führerbunker.

Trudle Junge @TJunge
The Goebbels' children have brought fresh life and vigor into the bunker. Each child was allowed to bring one toy.

Monday
23 April, 1945

Eva Braun (1912-1945)

Eva secretly indulges in a forbidden cigarette.

Longtime companion of Adolf Hitler and, for less than 40 hours, his wife; choosing to stay and die with her husband in the Führerbunker as Soviet forces closed in on Berlin and the Führerbunker.

Eva Braun @EBraun
The Führer is in a dark mood this morning despite my efforts to cheer him up.

Adolf Hitler @AHitler
Morell tried to give me morphine this morning. He and others may be attempting to knock me out so I can be transported to Berchtesgaden.

Wilhelm Keitel @WKeitel
I met General Wenck and told him that he and his 12th. Army can save Germany. He said he would do what he could.

Eva Braun @EBraun
The Führer has dismissed Doctor Morell and so has not received any medication today.

Adolf Hitler @AHitler
The business with Weidling was a misunderstanding. I have therefore appointed him Commander of the Berlin Defense Area.

Albert Speer @ASpeer
I am about to confess to the Führer that I have not carried out his orders for infrastructure destruction on Reich and occupied territories.

Hermann Goering@HGoering
I have sent a radiogram to Berlin expressing my willingness to assume overall command should the Führer be incapacitated, cut off, in Berlin.

Wilhel Keitel @WKeitel
I have just met with Speer who told me he is expecting his meeting with the Führer today to be his last.

Hermann Goering@HGoering

If there is no contact by 22.00 hours, I will assume my responsibilities in the Obersalzberg as the Führer's legal successor.

Martin Borman @MBorman
Soviet forces have taken Eberswalde without a fight. Steiner has refused to give the order for a full counterattack north of the city.

Hans Krebs @HKrebs
This afternoon, Goering has telegraphed that with the relocation of the military staff to the Obersalzberg, he is to take command.

Joseph Goebbels @JGoebbels
I have told the Führer that Reichsminister Goering is a traitor who is trying to stage a coup to seize power for himself.

Hermann Goering@HGoering
Still no reply from Berlin. If I do not receive a reply by 10 p.m., I will assume the Führer is incapacitated and take command of the Reich.

Hermann Goering@HGoering
I have sent the same message to Foreign Minister Ribbentrop (with a copy for Keitel). Still no reply from Berlin.

Albert Speer @ASpeer
While hearing that I had willfully ignored orders to implement Nerobefehl, the Führer, though angry, was surprisingly accommodating to me.

Alfred Jodl @AJodl
Reichsminister Goering has a point. Under the 1941 Decree of Succession, he is to assume command if the Führer is incapacitated.

Martin Bormann @MBormann
I have informed Goering that the decree only comes into effect on my specific agreement, and forbidden him to take any such treacherous steps.

Adolf Hitler @AHitler
I have stripped the pig Goering of all offices and expelled him from the Party. I will appoint von Greim to take command of the Luftwaffe.

Alfred Jodl @AJodl
Goering was dismissed due to the incitement of Bormann and Goebbels who see a way of getting rid of a hated rival for the Führer's affection.

Hermann Goering@HGoering
Having heard from Bormann, I have cancelled my previous message to Ribbentrop and Keitel.

Martin Bormann @MBormann
There can be no talk of lack of freedom to act on the part of the Führer. To do so is an act of treachery.

Hermann Goering@HGoering
Berlin informs me that my life will be spared, but I must resign all official positions. This I have done and expect to be arrested imminently.

Martin Bormann @MBormann
Foreign Minister von Ribbentrop has arrived in the Führerbunker requesting a meeting with the Führer. I have sent him away.

Helmuth Weidling @HWeidling
The Führer has tasked me with the defense of Berlin, with specific instructions not to surrender but to fight to the last man.

Joseph Stalin @Stalin
I have informed Zhukov that he is to take the government sector and the Chancellery. Marshal Konev is to stop 150m west of the Reichstag.

Helmuth Weidling @HWeidling
I would rather have been shot than have this final dubious honor of defending Berlin under such conditions.

Ivan Konev @Konev
Marshal Stalin has awarded the prize of Berlin to Zhukov. This despite my greater and more rapid advance for fewer losses.

Tuesday
24 April, 1945

Albert Speer (1905-1981)

Speer was a German Architect and Minister of Armaments and War Production for the Third Reich. A member of Hitler's inner circle, he was responsible for the design and construction of many of the Reich's iconic buildings, including the Reich Chancellery, as well as designing plans (with Hitler) to reconstruct Berlin on a grand scale.

Albert Speer @ASpeer
Yesterday, I said farewell to the Führer and made one last tour of the Chancellery before returning to Hamburg. Little is left of my work now.

Georgi Zhukov @Zhukov
We have severed the last remaining link between the German IX Army and the city.

Martin Bormann @MBormann
I have informed the Führer that the traitor and drug addict Goering is now under house arrest at his villa in Berchtesgaden.

Georgi Zhukov @Zhukov
Marshal Stalin has awarded my 1st. Belorussian Front the honor of raising the Soviet flag over the Reichstag just days from now.

Wilhelm Mohnk @WMohnke
The Führer has approved the establishment of an auxiliary airport for Berlin on the East-West axis.

Heinrich Himmler @HH
I have spoken by phone to Count Folke Bernadotte (Head of the Red Cross) re: terms of possible surrender to the Western Allies.

Reuters @DCReuters
In Italy, the Allies have encircled the last German armies near Bologna. The war in Italy is effectively at an end.

Walther Wenck @WWenck
I have disengaged from the Americans and am turning my army eastwards as per the orders from Keitel and the Führer.

Harry Truman @Truman

Secretary Stimson and General Groves are about to brief me with (finally) full details of the Manhattan Project.

Heinrich Himmler @HH
I am still awaiting a reply from Count Bernadotte regarding terms of a possible surrender of Reich forces.

Walther Wenck @WWenck
I have been in touch with General Busse and informed him of the plan to link our armies and attack the Soviets to the northeast.

Helmuth Weidling @HWeidling
Leading Soviet units continue probing and penetrating the S-Bahn defensive ring.

Alfred Jodl @AJodl
It now becomes clear that there is no prospect whatsoever of doing anything other than delaying the inevitable fall of the capital.

Richard Dimbleby @BBCDimbleby
The battle now taking place in Berlin will be recorded by history as the most horrific battle ever fought in a city.

Heinrich Himmler @HH
Western Allies have told the Red Cross to insist that any surrender of Reich forces must involve the Red Army. This is unacceptable to me.

Theodor Busse @TBusse
We are 80,000 men encircled in the Halbe pocket with only 79 combat-ready tanks and fewer than 1,000 guns and mortars remaining.

Hans Krebs @HKrebs
The western and eastern fronts are now so close that merely by turning his army around, General Wenck will be immediately facing the Soviets.

Theodor Busse @TBusse
To break out and meet up with the 12th. Army, we need to fight our way through 3 lines of the 1st. Ukranian Front. A very tall order!

Hans Krebs @HKrebs
General Steiner has been ordered to turn over his mechanized divisions to General Holste for his attack northwest of Berlin.

Walther Wenck @WWenck
We have successfully turned the 12th. Army around and my XX Corps are now attacking Soviet positions east and northwards towards Berlin

Theodor Busse @TBusse
I will push west like a caterpillar, with the King Tiger tanks of the 502 SS heavy Panzer battalion as the leading head of the caterpillar.

Eva Braun @EBraun
The Führer plays with the dogs for endless hours, often gazing thoughtfully at his portrait of Frederick the Great.

Hans Krebs @HKrebs
Wenck's immediate objective is the autobahn near Potsdam. Meanwhile, General Holste is to counterattack between Spandau and Oranienburg.

Martin Bormann @MBormann
The Führer is perhaps hoping for his own 'Miracle of the House of Brandenburg'. The miracle Goebbels assured him would surely come to pass.

Harry Truman @Truman
I am now fully aware of the details and implications of the Manhattan Project and the awesome responsibility which now falls upon me.

Wednesday 25 April, 1945

Traudl Junge (1920-2002)

Junge was Adolf Hitler's youngest personal private secretary from December 1942 to April 1945. She typed up Hitler's last private and political will and testament before escaping the Führerbunker and making it out of Berlin.

Trudl Junge @TJunge
This morning, a fine dust began entering the Führerbunker through the ventilation system. Breathing has become uncomfortable.

Harry S. Truman @Truman
I have received a memo from Acting Secretary Grew summarizing developments in Germany, France, Italy and Yugoslavia – all good!

Reuters @DCReuters
Forward units of Soviet and American troops have linked up for the first time at the river Elbe, near Torgau in Germany.

Helmuth Weidling @HWeidling
Over 2 million Soviet soldiers are bearing down on the capital that I promised the Führer I would defend to the last man.

Adolf Hitler @AHitler
The situation will improve! Busse and Wenck will bring the 9th. and 12th. Armies to Berlin!

Richard Dimbleby @BBCDimbleby
U.S. forces have blown up the swastika which stood atop the Zeppelintribuene Nazi Party Rally Ground in Nuremburg.

Harry S. Truman @Truman
Swiss Minister Stucki tells us that Hitler has fled Berlin for his reduit at Obersalzberg, presumably to make a last stand there.

The Times @TimesofLondon
Sources in the War Office warn that with the imminent fall of Berlin, there is a possibility of a protracted period of mountain warfare.

Martin Bormann @MBormann
I am informed that we no longer have forces in Milan following another unauthorized withdrawal. There is treachery everywhere.

New York Times @NYT
Fifty Allied nations have met in San Francisco at the opening of the United Nations Conference on International Organization.

Alfred Jodl @WJodl
Berlin Defense Sector C is coming under extreme pressure. I have appointed Krukenberg to take command.

Reuters@DCReuters
Berlin is now completely surrounded by forces of the Soviet Red Army with units penetrating into the city itself.

Walther Wenck @WWenck
I have been given authority to decide for myself the best direction of attack. This will make it easier for me to rescue the 9th. Army.

Hans Krebs @HKrebs
We have attempted air supply to the 9th. Army but the planes which were able to take off were unable to find the drop point.

Pravda @YuriPravda
The 1st. Ukranian Front has come under surprise attack by the German 12th. Army who appear to be attempting to break through to Berlin.

Hans Krebs @HKrebs
This evening, the Führer has recovered some of his optimism and issued further detailed orders to Generals Wenck and Busse.

Adolf Hitler @AHitler
I have ordered the 12th. Army to cut off the Soviet 4th. Tank Army and Busse is to hold onto his eastern front and attack westward.

Theodor Busse @TBusse
I have placed my HQ immediately behind the heavy tank battalion spearhead of the breakout to the west.

Adolf Hitler @AHitler
Once the 12th. and 9th. Armies are combined, they are to attack northwards to open a corridor through the Soviet encirclement of the capital.

Theodor Busse @TBusse
Colonel von Luck is to open a western corridor for the sole use of military units of the 9th. Army. No civilians are to be allowed to use it.

Richard Dimbleby @BBCDimbleby
The War Office reports that the RAF carried out a large raid today on the Obersalzberg complex, with many buildings substantially destroyed.

Theodor Busse @TBusse
This evening, my 9th. Army will make our first attempt to break out to reach Wenck's 12th. Army to the west of Berlin.

Thursday 26 April, 1945

Hermann Goering(1893-1946)

Goering was a German politician, military leader, and leading member of the Nazi Party (NSDAP). At one time, he was the second most powerful man in Germany and designated as Hitler's successor. Commander in Chief of the German Air Force (Luftwaffe), he was the only man to hold the rank of *Reichsmarschall*.

Hermann Goering @HGoering
The RAF have bombed the Obersalzberg complex where the SS are holding me under house arrest.

Wilhelm Keitel @WKeitel
The Muncheberg Division are continuing to hold Tempelhof Airport, but its capture by the Soviets now seems inevitable.

Hermann Goering @HGoering
The RAF may have bombed the Obersalzberg complex believing the Führer was with me at Berchtesgaden.

Richard Dimbleby @BBCDimbleby
Russian and American troops have joined hands at the River Elbe in Germany, bringing the end of the war a step closer.

Omar Bradley @Brad12th.Army
In 10 months, we have advanced 1,220 km from the invasion beaches to today successfully link up with our determined Soviet allies.

Hermann Goering @HGoering
I have persuaded my captor, SS-Obersturmbannführer Bernhard Frank, to move us to my castle at Mauterndorf.

Ivan Konev @Konev
It is clear that the German 9th. Army is not trying to break through to Berlin but is fleeing before us to reach the Americans at the Elbe.

Winston Churchill @Churchill
Our western and eastern armies meet today in true and victorious comradeship, with inflexible resolve to fulfill our purpose and our duty.

Walther Wenck @WWenck
There is no possibility of breaking through to Berlin. But we can create a route through which many of the 9th's troops can escape westwards.

Harry S. Truman @Truman
The hour draws near, the hour for which all the American people, the British people and the Soviet people have toiled and prayed so long.

Joseph Stalin @Stalin
Our task and our duty are now to complete the destruction of the enemy to force him to lay down his arms and surrender unconditionally.

Hans Krebs @HKrebs
I expected to meet Ritter von Greim arriving from Munich to take over the Luftwaffe but have heard he has been seriously wounded in transit.

Helmuth Weidling @HWeidling
I have located my HQ at the old army HQ on the Bendlerstrasse. It has well-equipped air-raid shelters and is close to the Reich Chancellery.

Vasily Chuikov @Chuikov
The 8th. Guards Army are through the suburbs in the south of the city and have attacked Tempelhof Airport.

Pravda @YuriPravda
In Berlin, pillboxes, barricades, mines, suicide squads with grenades clutched in their hands - all are swept aside before the Red Army.

Helmuth Weidling @HWeidling
Today I ordered Munchenberg to attack toward Templehof Airport with their last 10 tanks. Fierce defensive fire halted the attack.

Martin Bormann @MBormann
Goebbels has broadcast an announcement that Goering resigned due to his acute heart condition and that the Führer accepted the resignation.

Alfred Jodl @AJodl
In the battle around Baruth, tank-hunting teams have blown up several dug-in Soviet tanks.

Hans Krebs @HKrebs
Despite explicit orders to Wenck and Busse, not a single unit has so far broken through the Soviet lines to come to the aid of Berlin.

Heinrich Himmler @HH
I am still waiting for a reply from the Red Cross regarding my latest amended proposal for a ceasefire in the west.

Walther Wenck @WWenck
I ordered von Luck to stay near Baruth but discontinue his attack for the moment. However, he has disobeyed and disbanded his battle group.

Ivan Konev @Konev
Today we have captured a further 5,000 prisoners and 40 tanks south of Berlin.

Walther Wenck @WWenck
I have heard that after his battle group was disbanded (against my orders), von Luck's soldiers are attempting to break out individually.

Helmuth Weidling @HWeidling
Late this evening, I presented the Führer with a detailed plan for a breakout from Berlin. He turned it down flat.

Adolf Hitler @AHitler
There is no point in such a breakout. I have no intention of wandering around in the woods! I will stay here at the head of my armies.

Friday
27 April, 1945

Magda Goebbels (1901-1945)

Magda Goebbels was the wife of Nazi Germany's Propaganda Minister Joseph Goebbels. A prominent and devout member of the Nazi Party she was a close ally and supporter of Adolf Hitler.

Magda Goebbels @MGoebbels
The only bathtub in the bunker is in the Führer's quarters, and he has so kindly offered it for the use of all our 6 children.

Adolf Hitler @AHitler
Early this morning, I ordered the flooding of the Berlin underground to slow the advancing Soviets.

Helmuth Weidling @HWeidling
Krukkenberg has informed me that the Nordland Division will need to fall back to the Berlin center sector.

New York Times @NYT
Reports from Berlin say that hand to hand fighting between Red Army soldiers and German defenders is now taking place near the Reichstag.

Hans Krebs @HKrebs
Many of the Soviet tanks approaching the government sector are sitting ducks for our Hitler Youth squads and their Panzerfausts.

Wilhelm Keitel @WKeitel
The remnants of the Nordland Division have been pushed back into the central government district in Defense Sector Z.

Adolf Hitler @AHitler
Every day brings worse news from every sector in Berlin. My generals and senior officers are incompetents and cowards!

Alfred Jodl @AJodl
Nordland Division HQ has moved to the opera house. Hitler Youth attached to the division have destroyed 14 Soviet tanks with panzerfausts.

Vasily Chuikov @Chuikov
Units of the Waffen SS are the only professional units offering substantial resistance in Berlin now.

Helmuth Weidling @HWeidling
Everywhere the streets of Berlin are full of craters and broken brickwork. Every street and square lays desolate.

Hans Krebs @HKrebs
The Nordland's remaining eight Tiger tanks have taken up positions at the Tiergarten in support of Weidling's 56th. Panzer Corps.

Pravda @YuriPravda
This evening, Soviet troops have broken through strong German defenses in and around Berlin and cut Berlin off from the rest of the world.

Helmuth Weidling @HWeidling
The flooding of the Berlin underground has resulted in the drowning of hundreds of civilians and countless soldiers under my command.

Hans Krebs @HKrebs
The Führer has sent several messages to General Busse demanding that he turn towards Berlin. No reply has been received.

Martin Bormann @MBormann
It has become apparent that General Busse is attempting to break out west rather than come to the aid of Berlin.

Theodor Busse @TBusse
Our second attempt at a breakout to the west has failed. Colonel Pipkorn has been killed by Soviet tank fire and Colonel von Luck captured.

Dwight D. Eisenhower @Eisenhower
Our Red Cross contacts with Himmler reveal that, far from retreating to his reduit, Hitler remains in Berlin.

Saturday
28 April, 1945

Karl Doenitz (1891-1980)

Doenitz was Commander in Chief of the German Navy *(Kriegsmarine).* He was appointed by Hitler as his successor and given the titles of President and Supreme Commander of the Armed Forces following the death of Hitler.

Karl Doenitz @KDoenitz
Message from Bormann informs me that the Reich Chancellery is now a 'heap of rubble'. My heart weeps for the people of Berlin!

Wilhelm Keitel @WKeitel
Today I came across General Heinrici marching his troops AWAY from Berlin. He is guilty of treason, cowardice and sabotage!

Walther Wenck @WWenck
We have managed to break through and create a corridor from Halbe to the west, but have paid a very high price in losses of men and armor.

Karl Doenitz @KDoenitz
Bormann informs me of acts of treason among the OKW. Schoerner, Wenck and the others must immediately confirm their loyalty to the Führer.

Karl Doenitz @KDoenitz
I am informed of rumors that Reichsführer Himmler has been in contact with the Western Allies over the past few days.

Martin Borman @MBorman
The BBC are broadcasting news that Himmler has been trying to negotiate with the western Allies. If true, this will devastate the Führer.

Karl Doenitz @KDoenitz
I have contacted Himmler to ask if these rumors of surrender talks are true. He assured me that there is nothing to the rumors.

Hans Krebs @HKrebs
It has been confirmed to be true. Himmler has told the Western Allies the Führer will be dead within two days.

New York Times @NYT
The Italian dictator, Benito Mussolini, has been captured in Northern Italy while trying to escape with his mistress Clara Petacci.

Adolf Hitler @AHitler
Lorenz has handed me a dispatch of the latest BBC broadcast. It is true! Himmler is a traitor to the Reich and to me!

Adolf Hitler @AHitler
I have sent for Fegelein. He will know what Himmler has been doing. I demand a full accounting of Himmler's actions!

Eva Braun @EBraun
The Führer is in a terrible rage. He has sent for my sister's husband but nobody knows where he is.

Reuters @DCReuters
Mussolini, his mistress and other members of his puppet government have been shot and their bodies hung upside down in the streets of Milan.

Adolf Hitler @AHitler
I have ordered the immediate arrest of Fegelein who is surely aware of Himmler's treachery!

101 Airborne @101AirborneDivision
We have arrived at another concentration camp near Dachau. Nobody is left alive here, just hundreds of stinking corpses!

Adolf Hitler @AHitler
Himmler's attempt at surrender of the Fatherland is the worst, most heinous act of treachery in all history!

Eva Braun @EBraun
The Führer has ordered the execution of my sister's husband. I cannot say I think this wrong, but can only try to comfort dear Margarete.

Hans Krebs @HKrebs
I called Keitel at Supreme Command HQ in Furstenberg to tell him that if relief does not arrive in Berlin within 48 hours, all will be lost.

Wilhem Keitel @WKeitel
I assured Krebs that I would exert the utmost pressure to urge Generals Wenck and Busse to turn toward Berlin.

Theodor Busse @TBusse
Our battle plan is to continue moving west as fast as possible keeping the corridor towards the Americans open.

Walther Wenck @WWenck
Many of our younger soldiers in and around the town of Halbe are deserting, discarding their uniforms and donning civilian clothes.

Adolf Hitler @AHitler
Let it be known that I, as founder and creator of this movement, have preferred death to cowardly flight or even capitulation.

Theodor Busse @TBusse
Command and control in the Ninth Army has collapsed. There is no contact now between Ninth Army Headquarters HQ and Army Group Vistula.

Martin Bormann @MBormann
Late this evening, Field Marshal von Griem flew out of Berlin to Doenitz's HQ with instructions to arrest and deal with Himmler.

Sunday
29 April, 1945

Helmuth Weidling (1891-1955)

Weidling was the last commander of the Berlin Defense Area during the Battle of Berlin when he led the defense of the city against the advancing Soviet Forces, finally surrendering just before the end of World War II in Europe.

Helmuth Weidling @HWeidling
The Soviets have captured both Berlin airports. This puts a stop to the landing of airborne supplies for the capital.

Adolf Hitler @AHitler
Today I marry my loyal Eva. An official from Volkssturm will conduct the ceremony. Goebbels is to be my witness. Bormann the witness for Eva.

Reuters @DCReuters
All Axis forces in Italy have officially surrendered unconditionally this day at Caserta, in the Campania region of Southwest Italy.

Adolf Hitler @AHitler
Mussolini has been killed and publicly humiliated in Milan. Such ignominy must not befall the leader of the Third Reich!

Traudl Junge @TJunge
Eva is wearing the Führer's favorite dress, the black one with the roses at the neckline, and her hair is washed and beautifully done.

Eva Hitler @EHitler
Our marriage ceremony is complete. I foolishly started to sign my maiden name on the marriage certificate.

Richard Dimbleby @BBCDimbleby
U.S. forces have liberated Kaufering IV camp – another of the dozens of slave labor camps in the Dachau network.

101 Airborne @101AirborneDivision
We have brought in the mayor and townspeople of Hurlach to view the camp and ordered them to bury the corpses.

Traudl Junge @TJunge
Today I had the terribly sad duty of taking down the dictation of the Führer's last political and private testament.

Helmuth Weidling @HWeidling
My headquarters at Bendlerblock are now within meters of the front line. We are considering a breakout to the southwest.

101 Airborne @101AirborneDivision
The Mayor and townspeople of Hurlach claim to have known nothing of the functions of this concentration camp. We don't believe him or them.

Traudl Junge @TJunge
After typing up the Führer's last testaments, I joined the party for the Führer and Frau Hitler. We ate little sandwiches and drank champagne.

Gotthard Heinrici @GHeinrici
Keitel has accused me of treachery and cowardice. He has dismissed me and I am to be replaced by General von Tippelskirch.

Martin Bormann @MBormann
Following my advice, the Führer has stripped Himmler of all his Party and State offices, expelled him from the Party and ordered his arrest.

Helmuth Weidling @HWeidling
Soviet forces will be in the Reich Chancellery and over the Führerbunker by May 1st. at the latest.

Adolf Hitler @AHitler
I never wanted this war. It was orchestrated either by those of Jewish origin or working for Jewish interests.

Adolf Hitler @AHitler
I ask the government and the people to uphold the race laws to the limit and resist mercilessly the poisoner of nations - international Jewry!

Alfred Jodl @AJodl
Soviet forces are now less than half a mile from the Führerbunker.

Adolf Hitler @AHitler
I have signed the final succession documents. Copies made for Doenitz, Schoerner and the Brown House. All is complete.

Traudl Junge @TJunge
The Führer has announced that he and Eva will commit suicide in the coming hours.

Adolf Hitler @AHitler
I asked Shenke what would be the best method. He replied hydrogen cyanide. I already knew about this.

Helmuth Weidling @HWeidling
If the Führer approves, breakout will begin tomorrow night. We will try to link up with Wenck's army at the village of Ferch near Potsdam.

Adolf Hitler @AHitler
My trust in Himmler has now evaporated. I have therefore sent for Tornow and Professor Haase to come and test Himmler's capsules on Blondi.

Adolf Hitler @AHitler
I will not have it that the Bolsheviks take my body back to Moscow to exhibit in a cabinet of curiosities.

Traudl Junge @TJunge
Nearly everyone in the Führerbunker is drunk. The Führer does not seem to mind, even though he never drinks himself.

Adolf Hitler @AHitler
My beloved companion, the loyal Blondi, has performed her last service – dying for her Führer and the Fatherland.

Traudl Junge @TJunge
Those of us who have chosen to stay by the side of the Führer have been issued with cyanide pills.

Hans Krebs @HKrebs
I have requested the following: the whereabouts of Wenck's army, time of attack, location of 9th. Army and location of the breakthrough.

Traudl Junge @TJunge
Many of the secretaries in the Führerbunker have married officers this evening.

Adolf Hitler @AHitler
I will be cursed by history, but the responsibility for the outbreak of this war cannot rest with me. It must rest with international Jewry!

Monday
30 April, 1945

Vasily Chuikov (1900 – 1982)

Vasily Chuikov was a Soviet Lieutenant General in the Red Army during World War II. He commanded the Soviet forces in central Berlin and was the first Allied officer to learn of Adolf Hitler's suicide.

Vasily Chuikov @Chuikov
By this day's end, I expect to have taken the center of Berlin and planted the Soviet banner on behalf of Marshal Zhukov above the Reichstag.

Traudl Junge @TJunge
This day in the bunker begins within an atmosphere of finality and lethargy – a feeling I have never before experienced.

Martin Bormann @MBormann
I have radioed Doenitz to inform him that the Führer has appointed him as his successor in place of Goering.

Alfred Jodl @AJodl
Reply to Krebs: Wenck's spearhead bogged down. 12th. Army unable to move to Berlin. Bulk of 9th. Army surrounded.

Traudl Junge @TJunge
There is very little activity in the Führerbunker this morning. Many are still hungover from yesterday's party.

Wilhelm Mohnke @WMohnke
I have informed the Führer that Berlin center will not be able to continue to resist the Soviet onslaught for more than two more days.

Karl Doenitz @KDoenitz
Bormann states that the Führer is alive and that I am to proceed against all traitors. He continues to distrust the actions of Keitel.

Hans Krebs @HKrebs
There are reports that the Soviets have overrun the Tiergarten and one advance unit is on the streets next to the Reich Chancellery.

Helmuth Weidling @HWeidling
I told the Führer that the Berlin garrison will have run out of ammunition by this evening.

Karl Doenitz @KDoenitz
I received a strong message from Bormann complaining that the divisions in Berlin have been standing idle for several days. Hard to believe!

Vasily Chuikov @Chuikov
A Red Army assault team has reached the Reichstag. There is hand to hand fighting throughout the building.

Helmuth Weidling @HWeidling
This morning, I met with the Führer and informed him that the Soviets are now less than 500 meters from the bunker.

Adolf Hitler @AHitler
I have attended a final lunch with my loyal secretaries – spaghetti with a light sauce. Very good indeed!

Karl Doenitz @KDoenitz
I have asked Bormann to convey to the Führer that I will attempt to relieve him in Berlin, and to assure him of my unconditional loyalty.

Karl Doenitz @KDoenitz
But if fate compels me to rule the Reich, I shall continue this war to an end worthy of the unique, heroic struggle of the German people.

Helmuth Weidling @HWeidling
The Führer has now given me official permission to organize a breakout from the Führerbunker this evening.

Eva Hitler @EHitler
I did not attend lunch with the Führer today but have persuaded Traudl to leave the Führerbunker today and take my love to Bavaria.

Traudl Junge @TJunge
The Führer has taken his leave of us and retired with Eva to his private quarters – I fear for the last time.

Adolf Hitler @AHitler
At her own desire Eva goes as my wife with me into death. It will compensate us for what we lost through my work in the service of my people.

Otto Guensche @OGuensche
The Führer has given me a terrible order – but one I am compelled to obey.

Otto Guensche @OGuensche
I am to stand guard and allow no entry to the Führer's private quarters. Then to burn the Führer's body to deny the Soviets.

Trudl Junge @TJunge
I was playing with the children when I heard a shot, so loud, so close that we all fell silent. It echoed on and on through all the rooms.

Traudl Junge @TJunge
Otto has just informed us that the Führer and Eva are dead. Nobody is speaking.

Joseph Goebbels @JGoebbels
Bormann, Krebs and I have given our last salute to our beloved Führer – a tribute to his heroic flaming corpse.

Otto Guensche @OGuensche
Today, at 15.30, the Führer and his wife took their own lives. Their bodies were cremated in exact accordance with his orders.

Martin Bormann @MBormann
No units near Berlin have the capability to get through to the government sector now. The only course open is to attempt the breakout.

Magda Goebbels @MGoebbels
Our glorious idea is ruined, and with it everything beautiful and marvelous that I have known in my life.

Martin Bormann @MBormann
Krebs will tell the Soviet commander of the Führer's death so he can inform the Kremlin. We will attempt to arrange an armistice tonight.

Joseph Goebbels @JGoebbels
Following the heroic and selfless death of our beloved Führer, I now take over leadership in the bunker.

Georgi Zhukov @Zhukov
After 10 hours of hand to hand fighting through the 6 floors of the Reichstag, we successfully planted the Soviet red banner on its roof.

Tuesday
May 1, 1945

Harry S. Truman (1884-1972)

Harry S. Truman was the 33rd. President of the United States, succeeding to the presidency on April 12, 1945, following the death of President Roosevelt.

Harry S. Truman @Truman
I have received word from Marshal Stalin that the battle for Berlin is in its final hours.

Magda Goebbels @MGoebbels
The children are so happy down here in the Führerbunker. Everyone is so kind to them. What bliss for them to know so little of the world!

Joseph Goebbels @JGoebbels
General Krebs speaks Russian fluently. I have therefore tasked him with meeting with the Soviets to organize an armistice.

Karl Doenitz @KDoenitz
Goebbels and Bormann inform me that the Führer is dead. I am now Reich President; Goebbels - Reich Chancellor; Bormann - Party Minister.

Wilhelm Keitel @WKeitel
Krebs left the Führerbunker at 2 a.m. to contact the Soviet commander in Berlin and negotiate a ceasefire and armistice.

Hans Krebs @HKrebs
I have met with Marshal Chuikov who is commanding the Soviet forces in the center of Berlin and informed him of the Führer's death.

Hans Krebs @HKrebs
Our proposals for a ceasefire and armistice were met with derision and contempt by the Soviet commander.

Vasily Chuikov @Chuikov
Marshals Stalin and Zhukov have informed me that conducting negotiations is impossible. Only unconditional surrender will suffice.

Hans Krebs @HKrebs
The Soviets demand immediate and unconditional surrender. Something I am not authorized to agree to. I must return to the Führerbunker.

Joseph Stalin @Stalin
Marshal Zhukov has radioed that Hitler is dead. Goebbels and the Germans are asking for terms and conditions. What obscene vanity!

Martin Bormann @MBormann
Krebs returned from the Soviet position at 14.00. They have rejected our proposal for a ceasefire and armistice.

Magda Goebbels @MGoebbels
The children will sleep soon with the help of a sleeping draught Doctor Stumpfegger provided me. Then, it will be time.

Radio Berlin @RadioBerlin
The Führer's headquarters has announced that our Führer, Adolf Hitler, has died at his command post in the Reichchancellery.

Joseph Goebbels @JGoebbels
Krebs has returned to inform me that the Soviets demand unconditional surrender. My loyalty to the Führer forbids me from agreeing to such!

Magda Goebbels @MGoebbels
It is done! The children have left this world. A world denied the light of National Socialism is not a world worthy of such pure souls.

Joseph Goebbels @JGoebbels
Magda was so strong and brave to have ensured the children left without unnecessary pain. I only hope I can spare her any suffering also.

Radio Berlin @RadioBerlin
The Führer fought against Bolshevism until his last breath and died for Germany.

Radio Berlin @RadioBerlin
The Führer appointed Admiral of the Fleet Doenitz his successor. The Admiral and successor of the Führer will now speak to the German people.

Wilhelm Mohnke @WMohnke
The breakout from the Führerbunker will begin shortly. I have organized all remaining staff into small groups.

Martin Bormann @MBormann
This evening around 22.00, Reichminister Goebbels shot his wife in the Chancellery garden before turning his pistol on himself.

Martin Bormann @MBormann
General Mohnke has organized the breakout from the Führerbunker. The first group will leave at 23.00.

Karl Doenitz @KDoenitz
As successor to the Führer, it is my first task to save Germany from destruction by the advancing Bolshevik enemy.

Wednesday
May 2, 1945

Dwight D. Eisenhower (1890-1969)

During World War II, Eisenhower was the Supreme Commander of the Allied Forces in Europe. He had responsibility for planning and supervising the invasion of North Africa in 1942–43 and the successful invasion of France and Germany in 1944–45 from the Western Front.

Dwight D. Eisenhower @Eisenhower
The Nazis want a separate peace with the Western Allies in order to continue their war with the Soviets in the East. This will not happen!

Helmuth Weidling @HWeidling
After returning from meeting the Soviets, Krebs is in no shape to continue talks. I will go and meet with Marshal Chuikov myself.

Martin Bormann @MBormann
Generals Krebs and Burgdorf have shot themselves in the conference room. I shall shortly attempt to break out following the others.

Helmuth Weidling @HWeidling
After establishing my credentials, Marshal Chuikov asked me where Krebs was. I told him Krebs was about to commit suicide.

Vasily Chuikov @Chuikov
I asked General Weidling if he had actually seen the death of Hitler and Goebbels, or if he had only heard about it.

Helmuth Weidling @HWeidling
I told the Soviet Marshal that Generals Krebs and Bormann had informed me of the Führer's death.

Vasily Chuikov @Chuikov
General Weidling can issue a written order regarding complete surrender so his conscience will be clear in the event of continued fighting.

Helmuth Weidling @HWeidling
As instructed by Marshal Chuikov, I have issued a formal written order for the immediate cessation of resistance to the Soviet forces.

Vasily Chuikov @Chuikov
The meeting with General Weidling ended at 8.23 a.m., after which copies of his surrender orders were distributed to his remaining defenders.

Pravda @YuriPravda
Berlin falls to Red Army! Thus fell the once mighty capital, the defense of which cost Germany up to half a million men killed or captured.

Helmuth Weidling @HWeidling
With the demise of both the Führer and Reichminister Goebbels, the shameful duty fell to me to announce the capitulation of Reich forces.

Alfred Jodl @AJodl
General Weidling has sent sound trucks into the dark, early morning streets to announce the end of fighting.

Harry S. Truman @Truman
Now the two principal war criminals will not have to come to trial; and I am very happy they are both out of the way.

George Patton @Patton
Just heard the news of Hitler's suicide! I wanted to shoot that paper-hanging, son-of-a-bitch myself, but this will have to do.

Winston Churchill @Churchill
As we rebuild, we must remember: In war......resolution! In defeat......defiance! In victory......magnanimity! In peace......goodwill!

Pravda @YuriPravda
At 15.00 today, Red Army forces seized, entered, and secured the German dictator's fortified bunker under the Reichchancellery in Berlin.

Winston Churchill @Churchill
Today I can say, without hesitation, that the situation we currently face is definitely more satisfactory than it was this time five years ago.

(**Philip Gibson** @Philip Gibson)
Churchill did actually say that after responding to accounts that Berlin had fallen and that Hitler was dead... Such a wonderful understatement!

The End

(Please see 'Note from author' on next page)

Note from the author

Thank you for reading #Berlin45. I hope you found it both interesting and informative presented in this unique and experimental format. If you have any comments about the book, or suggestions for other historical subjects which you think might benefit from a similar approach, please feel free to email me with your thoughts at: arctraininglaos@yahoo.com.

If you have the time and the inclination, please consider submitting a review of #Berlin45 on its bookpage at the Amazon online store.

Thanks!

Philip Gibson
Vientiane
Laos

Major Sources

William Shirer. The Rise and Fall of the Third Reich (New York: Fawcett Crest, 1983; ISBN 0-449-21977-1)

Kershaw, Ian (2008). Hitler: A Biography. New York: W. W. Norton & Company. ISBN 978-0-393-06757-6.

Read, Anthony and Fisher, David; The Fall of Berlin, London: Pimlico, 1993. ISBN 978-0-7126-0695-0

Joachimsthaler, Anton (1999). The Last Days of Hitler: The Legends – The Evidence – The Truth. Brockhampton Press. ISBN 978-1-86019-902-8.

Donald L. Miller, The Story of World War II. Simon & Schuster, 2006. ISBN 0-7432-2718-2.

Beevor, Antony (2002). Berlin: The Downfall 1945. Viking-Penguin Books. ISBN 0-670-03041-4.

Heiber, Helmut, and David M. Glantz (eds.) (2004). Hitler and his generals. Military Conferences 1942–1945. New York: Enigma Books. ISBN 1-929631-28-6.

Shepardson, Donald E.; "The Fall of Berlin and the Rise of a Myth", The Journal of Military History, Vol. 62, No. 1.

Dallek, Robert (2008). Harry S. Truman. New York: Times Books. ISBN 978-0-8050-6938-9.

Manvell, Roger; Fraenkel, Heinrich (2007) [1965]. Heinrich Himmler: The Sinister Life of the Head of the SS and Gestapo. London; New York: Greenhill; Skyhorse. ISBN 978-1-60239-178-9.

Ziemke, Earl F. (1968). The Battle for Berlin: End of the Third Reich. New York: Ballantine Books. ISBN 0-356-02960-3.

Speer, Albert (1971) [1969]. Inside the Third Reich. New York: Avon. ISBN 978-0-380-00071-5.

Fest, Joachim (1999), Speer: The Final Verdict, translated by Ewald Osers and Alexandra Dring, Harcourt, ISBN 978-0-15-100556-7

Manvell, Roger (2011) [1962]. Goering. London: Skyhorse. ISBN 978-1-61608-109-6.
Evans, Richard J. (2008). The Third Reich at War. New York: Penguin. ISBN 978-0-14-311671-4.

CPSIA information can be obtained at www.ICGtesting.com
Printed in the USA
BVOW05s1039110314

347293BV00019B/1086/P